. . . LIFELINES . . .

New Baby Stress

...LIFELINES...

NEW BABY STRESS

DAVID & CLAUDIA ARP

Tyndale House Publishers, Inc.
WHEATON, ILLINOIS

Visit Tyndale's exciting Web site at www.tyndale.com

Copyright © 2003 by David and Claudia Arp. All rights reserved.

Cover photo copyright © by Getty One. All rights reserved.

Designed by Ron Kaufmann

Published in association with the literary agency of Alive Communications, Inc., 7680 Goddard Street, Suite 200, Colorado Springs, CO 80920.

Unless otherwise indicated, all Scripture quotations are taken from the *Holy Bible, New Living Translation,* copyright © 1996. Used by permission of Tyndale House Publishers, Inc., Wheaton, Illinois 60189. All rights reserved.

Scripture quotations marked NIV are taken from the *Holy Bible,* New International Version®. NIV®. Copyright © 1973, 1978, 1984 by International Bible Society. Used by permission of Zondervan Publishing House. All rights reserved.

Library of Congress Cataloging-in-Publication Data

Arp, Dave.
  New baby stress / David and Claudia Arp.
    p. cm. — (Life lines)
Includes bibliographical references.
  ISBN 0-8423-6008-5 (pbk.)
  1. Marriage. 2. Parents. 3. Communication in marriage. 4. Infants, Newborn—Care. I. Arp, Claudia. II. Title. III. Series.

HQ734 .A689 2003
649'.1—dc21   2002152200

Printed in the United States of America

07 06 05 04 03
7   6   5   4   3   2   1

. . . ABOUT LIFE LINES . . .

The Life Lines series is designed for *real* people in *real life* situations. Written by published authors who are experts in their field, each book covers a different topic and includes:

- information you need, in a quick and easy-to-read format
- practical advice and encouragement from someone who's been there
- "life support"—hands-on tips to give you immediate help for the problems you're facing
- "healthy habits"—long-term strategies that will enrich your life
- inspiring Bible verses
- lists of additional resources—books, Web sites, videos, and seminars to keep you headed on the right path

Life Lines is a joint effort from Marriage Alive International, Inc. and Smalley Relationship Center. Marriage Alive founders and directors David and Claudia Arp serve as general editors.

Whether you need assistance for an everyday situation, a life transition, or a crisis period, or you're just looking for a friend to come alongside you, Life Lines offers wise, compassionate counsel from someone who can help. This series will connect with you, inspire you, and give you tools that will change your life—for the better!

Titles in the series:
Life Lines: Connecting with Your Husband—Gary Smalley
Life Lines: Connecting with Your Wife—Barbara Rosberg

Life Lines: New Baby Stress—David and Claudia Arp
Life Lines: Survival Tips for Parents of Preschoolers—Becky Freeman
Life Lines: Communicating with Your Teen—Greg and Michael Smalley
Life Lines: Making Wise Life Choices—John Trent

*To all moms and dads who,
in the middle of new baby stress,
are seeking to find the time and energy
to love and support each other.*

. . . CONTENTS . . .

Introduction: What Happened to Life as You Knew It? . xi

1. The Toughest Job You'll Ever Love. 1
2. What It Means to Be Married with Kids 7
3. Life Support: Immediate Help for Surviving Today. 13
4. Healthy Habit #1: Sharing Responsibility and Working Together 33
5. Healthy Habit #2: Developing Healthy Sleep Patterns. 41
6. Healthy Habit #3: Finding Time for Each Other 47
7. Healthy Habit #4: Talking and Listening Effectively 53
8. Healthy Habit #5: Making Your Love Life a Priority 63
9. Healthy Habit #6: Growing Together Spiritually 71
10. Healthy Habit #7: Learning to Pace Yourself. . . . 79
11. Healthy Habit #8: Nurturing Your Relationship . . 85

Additional Resources. *91*

. . . INTRODUCTION . . .
What Happened to Life as You Knew It?

Do you ever wonder . . .

- what happened to those peaceful nights of sleeping soundly without one ear cocked to listen for a small voice?
- what happened to those pick-up-and-go days when you could hop in the car to run out for milk or bread—without car seats, strollers, or baby-sitters?
- what happened to those free-and-easy days when the only clean face, clean hands, and clean body you were responsible for were your own?
- what happened to that easygoing, smiling person you married once upon a time?
- if you'll ever pick up a newspaper or watch the evening news again without being interrupted?
- if you and your spouse will ever be able to carry on a whole conversation without one of you dozing off into an exhausted sleep?

We can still remember the day life as we knew it changed forever. Four years of "marriage on our own" were replaced with "marriage on demand." And all the demand was coming from our newborn son.

We both kept waiting for life to return to normal. It

. . .

never did. We waited for our love life to reignite, but instead our six-pound bundle of joy dynamited it. We waited for time to talk, time to sleep, time to take a shower. Nothing was working out like we thought it would.

I (Claudia) waited for David to say, "Honey, let me take over and change his diapers, walk the floor, rock him awhile"—anything that might soothe our colicky baby.

I (David) waited for Claudia to refocus on me.

We tried to convince ourselves, "Things will change when he gets on a schedule, when his digestive tract smoothes out, when he sleeps through the night, when he develops a happier disposition and doesn't cry so much, when . . . "

Things did change—they got worse. We went from being tired to being sleep-deprived. From being civil to each other to being short-tempered. From being competent people to being insecure and needy. Was this what it meant to be parents—to be perpetually crabby and discontent, and to discover that your spouse is a stranger?

Other parents experiencing new baby stress answer, "Yes!" Most new parents undertake this job with no previous training. And it's a job with an unusually challenging job description. What kind of courage would it take to apply for the following opening?

Who in their right mind would enlist for such duty?

> **JOB DESCRIPTION: PARENT & PARTNER**
>
> **Hours:** 24 hours a day; 7 days a week. No time off and night duty required
>
> **Responsibilities:** Love, cherish, and meet all your mate's needs; also feed, bathe, diaper, rock, walk, and whatever else is required to keep baby and spouse satisfied; light and heavy housework required
>
> **Future advancement:** Long-term commitment required; responsibilities may double or triple with additional children
>
> **Pay:** Be prepared to pay; typical added household expense for baby's first year can be as high as $10,000, and the cost of raising a child to the age of eighteen is estimated to exceed $200,000
>
> **Retirement benefits:** May be able to begin to save for retirement after college loans are paid
>
> **Commitment:** Lifetime

We did—and so did you. New baby stress is real, but also real are the many rewards that will come to you as parents. Psalm 127:3 says, "Children are a gift from the Lord; they are a reward from him." So take a break and spend the next few minutes with us as we offer you a life line for dealing with this wonderful but stressful time in your life.

NOTHING BUT THE TRUTH

In the following pages we will tell you the truth. We will tell you what to expect as new parents and how to make sure your marriage survives. We will concentrate on giving you life support—tangible "first-aid" tips for surmounting the challenges of new baby stress—and we'll direct you to helpful parenting resources. We'll also focus on some healthy habits—longer-term solutions that will enrich and strengthen your marriage relationship. And we'll share wisdom from the Scriptures from the One who created parenthood in the first place.

This book offers you immediate help! We've done the work for you. We have gleaned the best tips from researchers, experts in the field, and couples who have successfully made it through the new-parenting transition, as well as our own experience with our three sons, who are now parents themselves. We survived, they survived, and you can survive too.

If you are in the midst of that first year of parenting, you'll find practical ways you can regroup and unite for the days ahead. Among other things, you'll learn:

- How to prepare for the first weeks and months of parenting
- How to deal with lifestyle changes
- How to deal with stress and fatigue
- How to make time for each other
- How to communicate your needs and expectations
- How to share extra work and how to work together

- How to restart—and revitalize—your sex life
- How to grow together spiritually

The transition into parenting as partners is certainly one of life's greatest marital challenges. This book can be your lifeline and can help you energize your relationship while discovering the joys of parenthood. Hard work? Yes. But trust us, it's worth it!

... 1 ...

THE TOUGHEST JOB YOU'LL EVER LOVE

Heather and Luke were deep in the throes of the early days with their new baby—and they were melting down.

"I never dreamed how much having a baby would change our relationship," Heather complained. "Everything is turned upside down. For instance, when I went back for my six-week postpartum checkup, the doctor told me we could resume sex as usual. Who was he kidding? Sex was the last thing on my mind—plus, at that moment my greatest fantasy was eight hours of uninterrupted sleep!"

"Well, that wasn't exactly *my* fantasy!" said Luke. "But Heather's right. Everything has changed. I feel disoriented, insecure, and frazzled. I'm exhausted, too. And I wish resuming sex *was* on Heather's radar screen.

"I want to help," Luke continued, "but I don't know what to do. I don't know anything about infants. I've forgotten what it was like to have uninterrupted time to talk, to dream together, and just to hang out. It's like having a new job with no previous training and with no inkling of what might be required."

> *Two people can accomplish more than twice as much as one; they get a better return for their labor. If one person falls, the other can reach out and help.*
>
> ECCLESIASTES 4:9-10

We looked at Heather and Luke and smiled. They were new parents knee-deep in new baby stress, and they needed to learn how to pull together as a team. God created husbands and wives to be allies and teammates, not enemies. In Ecclesiastes 4:9-10 we read, "Two people can accomplish more than twice as much as one; they get a better return for their labor. If one person falls, the other can reach out and help." But when you're submerged in new baby stress, it's tough to see that and even tougher to make that teamwork happen. It takes time, work, and some wisdom to build a new life together. Together Luke and Heather can learn how to support and encourage one another in this most stressful time of life—and you can too!

WHEN PARTNERS BECOME PARENTS

Welcoming a new baby to your family is cause for celebration! This little one will bring you immeasurable joy in the years ahead. But he or she will also take much of your time and energy. Whether you become parents through birth or adoption, or even if you already have other children, the addition of a new baby introduces drastic lifestyle changes—especially in your marriage. How can you protect your relationship with your partner while experiencing the joy and hard work of parenting? Is it possible to survive the inevitable stress and fatigue that accompanies the birth of a new baby?

The challenges of becoming parents can be all-consuming, leaving parents little time to nurture their own relationship. Even if the marriage is strong and working well before children arrive, adjusting to a new baby adds stress and tension that can potentially tear a couple apart.

Marital researcher Dr. John Gottman, a professor at the University of Washington in Seattle, reports that

---

TOP FEARS OF NEW DADS

- Sex will never be as good again.
- We'll never recover financially.
- I'll lose all my guy friends.
- My wife's hormones will never settle down.
- My wife will never get back into shape.
- I won't be a good dad.

most couples experience eight times more conflict in their marriage after having a baby than before the baby was born. Most couples have no idea what kind of conflict lies ahead when they bring home that precious child. Dr. Gottman also relates that with the arrival of the first child, marital satisfaction drops in 67 percent of marriages. In the United States, 75 percent of couples who separate or divorce have a child between the ages of two and three years—and many report that the relationship began to weaken when the first baby arrived.[1]

So if you're finding the early days of parenting to be stressful, join the club! So do most couples. And if you're missing the relationship you used to have with your spouse, you're not alone. Studies on stress indicate that times of transition bring on the most pressure and tension. In their book *Becoming Parents,* marital researchers Pamela Jordan, Scott Stanley, and Howard Markman point out that becoming parents is considered the most significant of all life transitions.[2] The arrival of that new baby or adopted child signals a new era in your life— one that comes with major changes in your responsibilities and relationships.

> **Change in your relationship is inevitable, but well-managed change can work for your relationship rather than against it.**

The addition of a child involves some subtraction

. . .

as well. Spontaneity is a thing of the past. You can't go out to dinner or a movie on the spur of the moment, and running errands takes three times as long because you have to work around the baby's schedule. While the losses are well worth the trade-off, they are still losses—and it's natural for couples to deal with feelings of grief and sadness. Your old selves are gone—and so is your former lifestyle.

As you make this transition you can expect to have feelings of disenchantment and discomfort. During this time you may feel more vulnerable—and since your spouse is experiencing the same transition and feelings of loss or disenchantment, it's no wonder communicating suddenly becomes difficult. New baby stress affects your perspective, creating new feelings of protectiveness or defensiveness. Spouses may view each other in a more negative light than before this transition to parenting began.[3]

Many new moms and dads move beyond feelings of loss to feelings of fear—fears that their relationship may never be the same, that they'll never figure out this parenting thing, that the stresses will be too much for them.

HELP ME NOW!

In the early days of your new baby's life, it's easy to focus on your new parenting role to the exclusion of your partner role. But if you continue to focus only on your baby, your partner is sure to feel neglected and unsatisfied. And that drop in marital satisfaction is serious business. Your marriage needs help and attention right now—at a time when you have little energy or attention to bring to it.

But don't despair. Trust us, it's possible to avoid this negative syndrome and keep your relationship strong when you become parents. Change in your relationship is inevitable, but change—well-managed, of course—can work *for* your relationship rather than against it. You can find immediate life support right here in these pages as we offer you a life line for protecting and preserving your relationship.

... 2 ...

WHAT IT MEANS TO BE MARRIED WITH KIDS

In these days of heady emotions—heartfelt love, frustration, panic, you name it!—it's sometimes hard to step back and get a realistic, practical view of what you as a couple are up against. The prospects may be daunting, but let's take a clear look at the change from being a couple to being parents and the stress that comes with it.

PERSONAL CHANGES

With the arrival of a new family member, every facet of your life changes, starting with your own life as an individual.

Suddenly you're exhausted. You may struggle with

feeling insecure and inexperienced, wondering if you're really up to the task. You may feel overwhelmed as you look ahead to all the years of parenting this child. And even though you may feel lonely, you're never alone. That new baby is your constant companion. In the past you only had to relate to your spouse; now you must relate to two people and the baby comes first. This new person is totally dependent, and you're the parent!

If you've given birth, your most obvious changes are in your body. It has just gone through a traumatic experience, and you may be wondering if that body of yours will ever get back in shape again—any shape! Then, if you're breast-feeding, you begin to realize that your body is not your own. You are now a milk machine that doesn't always function smoothly.

> *[God's] compassions never fail. They are new every morning; great is your faithfulness.*
>
> LAMENTATIONS 3:22-23, NIV

If you're the dad, you also may feel insecure. While your body wasn't traumatized by childbirth, you're tired too. And if your wife is nursing, suddenly her body, which used to be available to you for pleasure, is employed around the clock as a twenty-four hour café for your baby.

Personal time—for play or reading or exercise—can feel like a vague memory. Sometimes it's a challenge even to get a shower before dinnertime. For both partners, roles and responsibilities are changing. The needs and demands of that tiny, dependent person make your life seem baby-centered, and it's easy to wonder if the marriage relationship will ever come back into focus at all.

MARITAL CHANGES

When the first baby arrives, your marriage typically transitions from a partner-focused relationship to a baby-focused relationship. Rhonda Kruse Nordin, in her book *After the Baby: Making Sense of Marriage after Childbirth,* points out that the baby "becomes the prism through which most new parents see the world"—and each other. The "time and energy [they] once devoted to strengthening their marital relationship is now redirected toward the new baby."[4]

Couple time is practically nonexistent. Communication patterns that worked BC (before child) no longer work. Your love life is on hold; whatever spontaneous fun you enjoyed in the past must now come as a result of planning.

Time and energy restraints are constant factors to deal with. No longer can you sleep through the night, watch a video (without falling asleep), eat a meal, or have a simple conversation without being interrupted. Fears of inadequacy, frustration, and feeling out of control may lead to anger and conflict.

. . .

Nine out of ten couples report that they argue more after becoming parents, and often their arguments center on unrealistic expectations about the care of the baby and the home. If one parent stays home with the baby, the working parent may expect the stay-at-home parent to take responsibility for all household chores. Wives and husbands may have differing assumptions about who will get up with the baby in the middle of the night, change diapers, or handle the extra laundry.

We very rarely argued before we had kids, but after our first child was born, we made up for it! We had just moved from Germany, the birth had been traumatic, and our son was colicky. We were exhausted and overwhelmed, and our stress level was high. Not surprisingly, we began snapping at each other over insignificant things. Leaving the milk carton on the counter or wet towels on the bathroom floor led to accusations that one of us wasn't doing our share of the extra work. Basically we felt out of balance.

Here's the good news: While parenthood can throw the marriage relationship into crisis, most couples are able to find a new balance in the first three to six months.

PROFESSIONAL CHANGES

"I'll never feel in control of my career again," a new mom told us. Her "after the baby comes" plan had been to become a consultant in her field, working part-time from home. Nothing was working! She had difficulty just coping with being a new mom and wasn't able to focus on her work. Professionally, she felt like a failure.

When one spouse cuts back, or stays home full-time, the financial dynamics change. Less money may mean less outside help. Seventy percent of new moms leave the workforce during the first year of motherhood, and some never return.[5] This can be the source of emotional as well as financial adjustments. A new mom who leaves her job to stay home with the baby may wonder who she is outside of her career. And sometimes the primary breadwinner must juggle the stresses of a job on four hours of sleep!

> When the first baby arrives, your marriage typically transitions from a partner-focused relationship to a baby-focused relationship.

For couples who continue to work, child-care issues become front-page concerns. Who will watch the baby? For how many hours a week? Other issues include things like which of you will take maternity or paternity leave? If that leave is without pay, how will you compensate? Can one or both of you work flexible hours?

HELP IS ON THE WAY!

New parents need help—life support, arm-around-the-shoulder help—right now! First, remember that God is

. . .

your ultimate source of strength and peace. He knows and cares about all the changes and stresses you're going through. When you need a reminder of that, read the great promises in Isaiah 41:10: "Don't be afraid, for I am with you. Do not be dismayed, for I am your God. I will strengthen you. I will help you. I will uphold you with my victorious right hand."

But God knows—and so do we—that sometimes the greatest comfort you can find is practical, hands-on, and tangible. We're here to give that to you! So read on for that life support.

...3...

LIFE SUPPORT: IMMEDIATE HELP FOR SURVIVING TODAY

When we ask couples their top marital stressors as new parents, the most common answers are "fatigue" and "just being overwhelmed." Other answers include "feeling out of control" and "just not knowing what to do." Some complain of a loss of freedom, or disappointment upon realizing that new baby care can be so all-consuming. Most admit that they focus so much on the baby's needs that their own needs are ignored and their marriage is suffering. New parents are rarely prepared for the impact a new baby has on their marriage.

CONTROLLING THE CHAOS

One new mom said, "I'm so stressed that I've lost my perspective. We wanted this baby for so long. Now she's here and I don't know what to do!"

These feelings are common. Even marriage and family specialists who are well-informed on this very subject struggle when they become new parents. Some friends of ours, both psychologists, struggled with feelings of inadequacy when their first baby was born. They say they have never felt more incompetent and helpless than they did the day they brought their baby home from the hospital.

> *The LORD is my strength and my shield; my heart trusts in him and I am helped.*
> PSALM 28:7, NIV

It's clear that new parents face a whole new set of challenges as they struggle to adjust to new roles and responsibilities. But there is hope. With a little understanding, communication, and planning, you *can* enjoy being parents and partners at the same time. So let's deal with fatigue first, and then we'll move on to feelings of inadequacy, confusion, loss of control, and misunderstanding.

DEALING WITH FATIGUE

Fatigue becomes the most pressing problem for new moms and dads. In order to find the energy necessary

. . .

to focus on your relationship with your spouse, you'll need to deal with your own individual fatigue first.

Before your child arrived, you probably slept for seven or eight hours at a stretch—and when you couldn't sleep, your spouse was nearby. You had that other person to talk to about the stresses or ideas running through your head, to snuggle with, or to rub your aching back. How things have changed! Now you're both coveting sleep and grabbing it whenever you can. With a baby constantly waking you up, the last thing you want to do in the middle of the night is invest in your relationship.

And those wake-ups *are* constant! Some newborns only sleep two hours before it's mealtime again. And we're not talking three squares a day, either. Newborns may need to be nourished every two or three hours around the clock. Whether or not your newborn is breast-fed, you and your spouse will be up at night. Even if he's not involved in the feeding, Dad's sleep is often disrupted as well if he's involved with placating a

---

TOP FEARS OF NEW MOMS

- I'll never lose the weight I gained.
- I'll never be sexy again.
- My husband won't think of me sexually in the same way.
- I'll never get rested again.
- I won't be a good mom.
- My body will never heal.

very awake baby or changing diapers. Very few new parents, husbands or wives, sleep uninterrupted through the night. No wonder exhaustion is typical.

Thank goodness that new baby is so darling and charming, or parents would have a tough time hanging in there through this difficult period of deprivation of a basic, fundamental need—sleep. Exhaustion definitely impairs your ability to function, and it can wreak havoc on your relationship with your spouse. When you're tired, tempers flare and you lose your ability to look at things from each other's perspective. Misunderstandings are likely, and when you combine misunderstanding with a short fuse—*kaboom!* Your communication and conflict resolution skills can easily become strained as you view everything through the filter of exhaustion.

> As you and your spouse begin to parent together, each of you comes to the project with differing expectations for yourselves and for each other.

Give yourself a break
Run through this list of practical suggestions. Which ones could help you immediately, even today?

1. **Reevaluate your expectations.** Which time-consuming home and family tasks are really essential, and which could be put off or eliminated?

Recognize that your before-baby expectations for housecleaning, personal time, couple time, and hours for concentrating on professional work are no longer realistic or helpful. Let go of guilt and frustration about the things you aren't able to get done. Sweep the kitchen floor once a week instead of twice. Make a supper of grilled cheese and a can of soup instead of duck à l'orange with wild rice pilaf. Pick the big stuff off the floor and vacuum tomorrow. Lower your expectations and feel successful if you make it through the day!

2. **Narrow your focus.** For now, focus on just four things:
   - your baby's safety and well-being
   - keeping yourself as sane and rested as possible
   - staying emotionally connected with your spouse
   - keeping the home going with the bare minimum of household chores (groceries, laundry, dishes).

3. **Sleep when your baby sleeps.** This may seem like a no-brainer, but for many new parents, those precious moments of freedom are viewed as a chance to leap into hyperdrive and tackle dirty floors, e-mail, or computer projects. Just say no to that impulse. When the baby is napping, don't do anything. Stretch out and get some zzzzz's. If you have difficulty sleeping in the daytime—even when you're totally exhausted—make yourself lie

. . .

down with a good book or magazine and you'll probably drop off to sleep. Even if you don't sleep, the quiet time alone will be good for you and you'll get some much-needed rest.

4. **Get some help.** Ask your spouse, a relative, or a neighbor to relieve you for an hour or two so you can sleep. If necessary, hire a neighborhood teenager or a nanny to give you a daily break. If you belong to a local church, now is the time to speak up about your need for rest. An older, retired woman might enjoy cuddling your little one for the afternoon—or might even stay overnight once or twice to give you a break. Other parents will empathize and be willing to help because they've "been there" and can remember those days of exhaustion.

Teens from your church family also may be interested in helping with baby care and house keeping jobs on a short-term basis.

Even if you are not currently part of a local church, you can still call on the church for help—if only to put a notice on their bulletin board. Your local high school or a college might have a job-placement office where you could advertise for paid positions.

> *Those who wait on the LORD will find new strength. They will fly high on wings like eagles. They will run and not grow weary. They will walk and not faint.*
>
> ISAIAH 40:30-31

. . .

5. **Get proper nutrition.** Vitamins, eight glasses of water, and lots of fruits and vegetables every day can make a real difference in your energy level. If you are a nursing mother, be sure to keep plenty of calcium (from milk, yogurt, broccoli, cauliflower, etc.) in your daily diet.
6. **Exercise.** Push the baby in a stroller or work out for at least fifteen to thirty minutes each day. It will benefit both of you. While this may seem like a personal indulgence that should fall in your list of priorities somewhere after cleaning your house, it's not! Exercise is energy-boosting, although it may initially seem energy-draining.

   Exercise with the baby in plain view in his bouncy seat or bassinet. Later, you might find some parent-and-baby exercise videos that make your exercise regimen a much-loved playtime with your baby. It's more fun to lift your growing little one than to heft weighted barbells.

   Another ideal exercise option is to take a daily

HEALTHY SNACKS

- Raw vegetables with low-fat dip
- Fruits such as oranges, apples, and bananas
- A glass of low-fat milk
- Raisins and nuts
- Low-fat yogurt
- A tall glass of ice water with a slice of lemon or lime

evening walk around the neighborhood after dinner with your spouse. Your baby will enjoy accompanying you in her stroller. If the weather is inclement, ask a neighbor to watch the baby. This is one more way to snatch some couple time while you're getting much-needed exercise. As much as your body needs that workout, your marital relationship depends on that chance to talk and connect emotionally.

FEELING OVERWHELMED

Remember Luke, who felt that becoming a parent was like getting a new job he was totally unqualified for? Many parents feel unprepared and afraid as they realize the multiple and varied tasks child rearing requires. Very soon after the baby is born, parents discover that instructions don't come with the baby's birth certificate. During the nine months of pregnancy, most new parents busy themselves with learning about the pregnancy and preparing for delivery. Decorating the nursery and procuring needed baby equipment typically consume more time than actual preparations for parenthood. Prenatal classes help you learn how to breathe and how to coach your partner through a successful labor and

> Even though you're tired and busy, talking with your spouse needs to stay at the top of your priority list.

delivery, but not many prepare you for what comes after that.

The huge and unrelenting responsibility of caring for a newborn overwhelms most new parents. It's common to experience feelings of inadequacy and incompetence. But don't despair. The following steps can help you to feel more assured and capable immediately.

1. **Invest in good resources.** There are lots of good parenting books out there, some offering a broad range of information and others written to address specific problems and situations you might experience. If you can't get to a bookstore, the bookstore can come to you. Try using an on-line bookstore like Amazon.com. Here's a list of books we recommend:

   General child development:
   What to Expect the First Year by Arlene Eisenberg, Heidi Murkoff, and Sandee Hathaway. This sequel to the widely used *What to Expect When You're Expecting* is quickly becoming a standard.

   Child Behavior by Frances Ilg, Louise Bates Ames, and Sidney Baker. This is the classic child-care manual from the Gesell Institute of Human Development.

   Complete Book of Baby and Child Care by Focus on the Family. A comprehensive guide to child rearing from birth to the teenage years, including an emergency-care section.

Balancing the new baby with your marriage:
Becoming Parents by Pamela Jordan, Scott Stanley, and Howard Markman. This resource deals primarily with the effects of parenting on marriage.

After the Baby by Rhonda Nordin. Another resource for couples focusing on the marriage relationship as it changes after childbirth.

2. **Call a friend.** You probably have friends or acquaintances who also have a baby or toddler. They're going through the same things you are and may be just a little farther along the parenting road. When you've got a question (or a full-blown panic attack!), call and ask.

3. **Find a mentor couple.** Do you know couples that seem to have struck a good balance between their roles as partners and their roles as parents? Ask them to become official mentors for you, intentionally spending time with you—with and without your child—for the purpose of observing and advising.

   It's great to have people around you who have gone before you and have gotten it right. They can give you many helpful and practical tips that will make a real difference in your marriage relationship. Maybe they figured out a good way to divide feeding duty or devised a creative plan for dealing with a colicky baby. They may be able to reassure you that your conflicts and questions are perfectly normal. Your church family is the ideal place to find such an experienced couple, or perhaps there is a relative or coworker who would fit the bill.

> **Keep a pad on your desk or kitchen counter and write down your parenting questions as you think of them. Then the next time you talk to a more experienced friend, you'll know what you want to ask.**

4. Join a new-parents' support group.

Often parent support groups are formed from prenatal preparation classes. Check with your church or community services. Ask other new parents if they know of such a group. If you can't find one, you may want to start your own. Some groups bring in experts to discuss a specific topic every week, offering practical advice and information you'll need as new parents. Other groups focus more on sharing and support. Either way, spending time with other new parents is important because you'll see that you're not alone. Sometimes it helps just to know that others are struggling with the same feelings or situations as you.

Postpartum depression

More than half of all new moms experience some form of postpartum depression in the days and weeks following the birth of their baby. This can be attributed to a number of physical and emotional factors. These include:

- Exhaustion and pain of labor and delivery
- Blood loss during and after delivery
- A dramatic shift in hormone levels following delivery
- Loss of sleep
- Frustration due to nursing problems
- Worry about the baby, especially if there are medical problems
- A feeling of being overwhelmed

Symptoms of postpartum depression can occur without warning and are as varied as the individuals who suffer from it. Common symptoms include irritability, tearfulness, anxiety, insomnia, lack of energy, loss of appetite, or difficulty concentrating.

Usually these "baby blues" dissipate on their own as a mother's hormone levels begin to even out. Moms, you can alleviate some of the pressure by getting lots of rest. Don't be afraid to seek support from your spouse, family members, and friends.

If the depression lasts longer than two weeks and the symptoms are becoming more severe, it may be a sign of a more serious problem. If you find that your emotional state is interfering with your ability to care for your baby, it's important that you talk to your doctor immediately. He or she can properly diagnose the problem and offer treatment options to get you back on the path to health more quickly.

REGAINING SOME CONTROL

Many new fathers and mothers often find themselves asking, "Where did my life go? I have no time for me! My life is out of balance. Will I ever feel in control again?"

The answer is no—and yes. Your life will never be as simple and controllable as it was before you added a new baby to the mix. Balancing your roles as parents and partners is one of the most difficult tasks you'll face as a couple, especially when there are so many other pressing problems to deal with first—changing diapers, for example. It's hard to imagine that you'll ever regain a feeling of being in control. But you and your spouse can and will restore equilibrium. And the way to begin is to create some balance in your own life first.

. . .

When you get on an airplane, the flight attendant explains the emergency procedures, including, "In case of emergency, put the oxygen mask on yourself before attempting to help others." The same principle applies to parenting. In order to be the best help for your spouse and your child during this "parenting emergency," it's important that you pay special attention to your own emotions and activities first. Try a few of these emergency action steps:

1. Take deep breaths and count to ten. You may not have stopped to breathe all day!
2. Sit down and have a cup of herbal tea or a glass of lemonade.
3. Read a few pages in a book or magazine.
4. Go on-line and browse for books with health tips for busy people. Order one you'd like to read. You might even find a little time to dip into it!
5. When the baby is sleeping, abandon the housework and take a nap or a long, relaxing bath or shower.
6. Hire a baby-sitter for a couple of hours and take a nap. Do nothing.
7. Take a short walk.
8. Get your hair cut in an easy-to-care-for style.
9. Call a friend and chat for a few minutes.

10. Bring home your favorite video and plan a home video date. Give yourself and your spouse permission to fall asleep at any point during the movie.

OVERCOMING MISUNDERSTANDINGS AND LONELINESS

As you and your spouse begin to parent together, each of you comes to the project with differing expectations for yourselves and for each other. Each of you has an idea of what you need and how you think your partner should help you. Is it any wonder there are often misunderstandings and hurt feelings?

New mothers may feel insecure, unprepared, and uncertain in their new role. They often want assurance that they're doing a good job and long for their husbands to be ultra-sensitive to their feelings. A new mom wants to know she is loved and appreciated. She also needs to know that she is still physically attractive.

New fathers are also thrown into new territory. They're looking for respect and their wives' approval and acknowledgment of their contribution to the family.

What are you expecting from your spouse? Whatever your expectations may be, you can bet that they're different from your spouse's.

A young woman we know named Rita grew up in a home where her parents handled the tasks of parenting as a team. Rita's mother was a successful interior decorator, and her father was a college professor. From her earliest memories, Dad was just as involved in Rita's life as Mom was. In fact, he was the chef and enjoyed preparing most of the evening meals. On many evenings he was the one overseeing bedtime prayers and tucking Rita into bed, while Rita's mother was busy with evening appointments with her clients. It's no surprise that Rita assumed that her husband, Will, would take on many of the roles her father had. However, Will grew up in a totally different family lifestyle.

> *The steps of the godly are directed by the LORD. He delights in every detail of their lives. Though they stumble, they will not fall, for the LORD holds them by the hand.*
>
> PSALM 37:23-24

Will's dad was a heart surgeon; his mother was a stay-at-home mom who invested most of her time in Will and his two brothers. Will's dad put in seventy-hour weeks at the hospital. When he could be at home, Will's dad was great. He was involved with the family and considered his time with the boys as far more valuable than nine holes on the golf course. But Will's dad had confidence that his wife could handle most of the parenting decisions and the day-to-day family routine on her own. Will came into his own days of fatherhood with that picture of what normal family life should be, although he felt a strong desire to be more available to his family than his dad had been.

So both Rita and Will came into parenting with expectations of how things would work. Their expectations were quite different and, as you can imagine, there were plenty of disappointments and misunderstandings ahead for them.

When Will changed just one diaper or folded a load of clothes, he felt proud that he had really made a sacrifice. Meanwhile, Rita was thinking, *One lousy diaper! One load of laundry, out of fifteen per week!* Rita felt upset that Will wasn't willing to carry more of the parenting load. She wished he would at least take over

---

LIFE ENERGIZERS

1. Lower your expectations for what you can accomplish in a day.
2. Reward yourself. For instance, take a bubble bath by candlelight, eat a bowl of ice cream, or watch a video that always makes you laugh.
3. Tips for quick dining: Buy frozen dinners. There are lots of convenience foods available now—try them! Use your microwave to heat foods quickly.
4. Stock up on disposable diapers, wipes, and extra formula for emergencies—even if your baby is primarily breast-feeding.
5. Drink eight glasses of water each day.
6. Listen to a favorite CD.
7. Take vitamins.
8. Make a to-do list and then cut at least half the items.

kitchen duties. Rita and Will were bound to stay disappointed with each other unless they talked openly about their ideas of family life and their expectations.

So even though you're tired and busy, talking with your spouse needs to stay at the top of your priority list. It's critical that you communicate your needs and expectations to your spouse. Talk about changing roles and responsibilities. Talk about how you can divide up the extra work and how you can work together as a team. Acknowledge how your lifestyle is changing right now. Nordin offers this survival tip: Go beyond your differences and say to each other, "Let's put our heads together over this one." She encourages couples to discuss issues with mutual respect, trust, communication, and cooperation despite their differences.[6]

> **Even though you're tired and busy, talking with your spouse needs to stay at the top of your priority list.**

After our third son was born, I (David) assumed the major responsibility for putting the two older boys to bed, which included a fun bath time with Dad, several bedtime stories, numerous potty runs before lights were out, and bringing ten glasses of water before the boys were settled. Claudia appreciated a few quiet moments and didn't mind taking on the responsibility of tidying up the kitchen. Often she would call her mom or a friend and chat while she loaded the dishwasher. Some evenings the dishes didn't get done and the boys didn't get baths, but generally our responsibility-sharing plan worked well.

BUILDING A STRONG FOUNDATION

You've been feeling tired, inadequate, out of control, and maybe even misunderstood. But we hope you can now see there are stabilizing helps that can go to work—immediately—to get your dual roles as partners and parents into the right groove. Cultivating your relationship is so important that we're turning next to the topic of healthy marital habits you can develop for the long haul.

Maybe in your pre-baby days, you and your spouse had already built a strong foundation of healthy marital habits. If so, congratulations! But now that the "earthquake" of a new individual in the family has shaken your foundation, it's time to rebuild in order to balance the dual roles of partner and parent. While you're adapting to the challenges of parenting, there's almost nothing more important than keeping your friendship, intimacy, and love growing.

Obviously, healthy marriage habits begin with finding time for each other, and this is certainly a challenge now that you are three—or more. For us, we found ourselves having to regroup and reclaim time for each other after each of our babies arrived.

. . .

In the next chapter, we'll talk about ways you can reconnect with your spouse. Let's start by looking at how to develop the habit of approaching parenting as a team.

... 4 ...

HEALTHY HABIT #1: SHARING RESPONSIBILITY AND WORKING TOGETHER

Nothing challenges teamwork more than having a baby! Many couples take prenatal classes and function as a team in the delivery room. Our advice? Bring that team spirit home with you from the hospital—especially if you want your marriage to survive and thrive in the coming days, weeks, and months. Maybe you have shared responsibilities in the past, but if your approach to life's work was more divide-and-conquer, now is the time for a new beginning.

SIDE BY SIDE, HAND IN HAND

This parenting journey is a long one, and there are many, many big and small jobs to tackle before you reach your journey's end. If you and your spouse are going to make it for the long haul, you need to be able to work together.

Schedule a working-out-the-work session where you can sit down and talk through all the jobs and responsibilities currently needed to keep your life going. What tasks were there all along? Can those responsibilities stay the same, or do you need to rethink who will take care of them? Which ones are new, specially delivered with your new arrival? Divide these chores, getting clear on which of you is going to handle what, and which tasks you'll share.

> As God's chosen people, holy and dearly loved, clothe yourselves with compassion, kindness, humility, gentleness and patience. Bear with each other and forgive whatever grievances you may have against one another.
>
> COLOSSIANS 3:12-13, NIV

In one survey, three-fourths of the women interviewed felt they received inadequate help from their husbands with child care and housework.[7] This can be a big source of stress and resentment, so look carefully at how you divide these tasks. Realize that moms who stay at home with the baby can make only limited use of this time for housework and errands. Don't assume that she can do the majority of household work because she's not working outside the home.

Once you get your list, you may find that there are more tasks than any two human beings can feasibly handle. Together, analyze your resources. Can you afford to have a cleaning service once a week? Every two weeks? Even once a month could be a big help. Do you share food-preparation responsibilities? Can you temporarily afford more convenience foods or take-out than you've been accustomed to using? Does your grocery store offer a shopping service via the Internet—and will they deliver to your house? One couple we know who are both attorneys hired a personal chef for the first few weeks after their baby was born. While this may be out of your budget, maybe your friends would divide the days and give you a gift of being your personal chef for a week.

Sharing responsibility and working together involve more than keeping the house clean and food on

---

WHAT EACH PARTNER NEEDS FROM THE OTHER

- Involvement and support
- Help with household chores:
  Cooking
  Dishes
  Cleaning the bathrooms
  Cleaning the kitchen
  Picking up toys, newspapers, baby items, etc.
  Laundry
  Vacuuming
  Dusting
  Running errands
- Appreciation and encouragement

the table. Here are some ideas to help reinforce your teamwork when it comes to handling all the family logistics.

FAMILY CALENDAR

Create a schedule for your marriage and family. If you want to have some sense of being in control, you need to take the initiative and create your own schedule. Start with a blank calendar. Write in the things that are not flexible—like work hours and other obligations. Then claim some time for your marriage. If you write in time for the two of you on your schedule, you'll be more likely to have it! Then add a tentative family schedule, including chores and household responsibilities. A tip: Leave lots of white spaces! Don't fill up all your time. Babies are unpredictable, and they, too, require lots of time.

Place your calendar in the kitchen or a place where you can see it. Then use your calendar to coordinate your schedules. Just having a tentative schedule, even if you can't follow it exactly, will be a great help!

A STYLE FOR THE TWO OF YOU

It's not just household responsibilities that need negotiating; it's also parenting responsibilities! You're suddenly faced with many decisions about how to care for this little one, and the two of you need to agree about nitty-gritty issues you may never have considered before.

What to do? Talk about parenting issues ahead of time. So many arguments would be avoided if new parents would just talk together and agree how they will approach certain concerns. Here are some questions that will help you get started with finding your own parenting style:

- Who will support the family financially? Will both continue to work?
- Have we checked out maternity and paternity leave? Who will take it?
- What is acceptable child care?
- Where do we want our baby to sleep?
- Who will get up with the baby at night?
- How will our baby be fed? Breast-feeding or formula? For how long?
- How important is it to us to have our baby on a predictable schedule?
- How can we work together so that we can each get some rest?
- When and who will we use for baby-sitters?
- When and where will we take our baby? Shopping? To the church nursery? To a restaurant?
- How do we feel about discipline? What types of discipline are appropriate?

- How do we want to relate to grandparents?
- Will we leave our baby with relatives?
- What will be our standards for household tasks? How do we define "a clean house"?
- How should we distribute household chores and responsibilities?
- What will the bedtime routine include? Will we ever let the baby "cry it out" so she learns to sleep on her own?
- If you are both going to be working, when will the child start day care? How will you decide on a day-care provider?
- What are the parenting issues we will likely face in the next twelve months? For example, what items and rooms in our house will be off-limits to the baby? What steps will we need to take to childproof our home? Do we have concerns about the baby's interaction with our pets? Are we in agreement with how we will approach the upcoming stages?

IT TAKES TWO, BABY

There was a very good reason that God's plan for families included two parents—there's plenty of work to go around, for one thing! You and your spouse can sidestep many argument land mines by talking through the many responsibilities and day-to-day tasks that are part of the new landscape of your life as partnering parents. And having worked this out opens the door for natural conversations over new tasks that come up or problems in your original division of labor. Keep on talking about it—and take a minute to put down the dishrag for a hug.

> There was a very good reason that God's plan for families included two parents—there's plenty of work to go around.

... 5 ...

HEALTHY HABIT #2: DEVELOPING HEALTHY SLEEP PATTERNS

To overcome the energy crisis, you need sleep—and for you to get sleep, your baby needs to sleep! You need to develop personal sleeping habits that will revive your energy and give you the strength to carry on. But in order to accomplish this, you need to do what you can to work toward healthy sleeping patterns for both you and your baby.

SLEEP ON IT!

The authors of *Becoming Parents* point the way toward good sleep patterns for parents. The following recommendations are adapted from their advice.[8]

Establish a regular sleep pattern. Evaluate your

typical sleep pattern. What time do you prefer to go to bed? What time do you usually get up in the morning? How many hours do you typically sleep? You may realize that you were already sleep deprived before the baby arrived! And even if you were getting enough sleep before the baby, you probably aren't getting adequate rest now. So take a close look at your sleep habits and see what unhealthy habits you may need to replace with healthy ones.

> [Jesus] said to them, "Come with me by yourselves to a quiet place and get some rest."
>
> MARK 6:31, NIV

Do you have a TV in your bedroom? Do you catch yourself turning it on when it would be better for you to get to sleep? If you don't want to miss that late-night program, use your VCR to record it, and view it at another time. Once you've discovered the areas that need improvement, make a commitment to change your sleep habits for the better.

Take naps or, if you can't take naps, take rests. In the first months of parenting, napping can make a big difference in how you manage fatigue. Sleep experts recommend taking power naps of twenty to thirty minutes midday, if possible. A caution: naps longer than one hour or within three hours of bedtime may interfere with your sleep at night.

Get regular exercise. If you are going to make just one change in your behavior, experts recommend that it be to get exercise. Just a few minutes of exercise each day can increase your energy level and will help you sleep better at night.

Establish a bedtime routine. This may be easier said than done, but at least give it a try. Maybe you will want to take a warm bath, listen to relaxing music, or indulge in a cup of herbal tea. Do whatever helps you to relax. Avoid stimulating activities or dealing with issues and problems right before you go to bed.

Naturally, it's a good idea to begin early to get your baby established on a bedtime routine. But, honestly, some babies don't cooperate as well as others! And parents differ as well. Some parents thrive on routine and structure; others are more free-spirited and prefer to let the baby set his own schedule. However you approach the bedtime-routine issue, we encourage you to be intentional and talk about what will work best for you.

Create an environment that supports sleep. Sleep experts recommend keeping the room temperature between sixty and sixty-five degrees Fahrenheit for sleeping. They also recommend the same temperature for the baby's room. You and your baby also need a quiet place to sleep. If it's impossible to block out noise, try using a humming fan, a humidifier, or some other sound machine that generates

> **To overcome the energy crisis, you need sleep—and for you to get sleep, your baby needs to sleep!**

. . .

white noise. This can work well for both parent and baby.

For years we have used a sound machine; we take it with us when we travel. And we can tell you firsthand that it works! Experts also suggest that no lights be left on during sleep time, except perhaps a nightlight in the hall.

WHERE WILL BABY SLEEP?

We have referred to the baby's room, but some parents choose to keep the baby in their bedroom for a period of time. This is a personal decision. Sometimes the baby is in the parents' room because of space constraints. Other parents enjoy the feeling of closeness and security that can come from having the baby in the same room. Many parents choose to put the baby in her own room and use a baby monitor. However, some parents find that the baby monitor keeps them awake even more because they tune in to every little sound the baby makes while sleeping.

Where the baby sleeps is a personal decision that you'll need to make for your family. Whatever you choose, however, do so with the intention of creating the best rest possible—for you and for your baby. If having the baby in the room with you makes it difficult to sleep soundly, move him to his own room. Don't worry, you'll still hear him!

. . .

No doubt you can hardly wait until that very good morning when you wake up and know—immediately—that you've just slept through the night! Until then, do everything you can to work toward that day and to keep your mind and body as rested as possible.

... 6 ...

HEALTHY HABIT #3: FINDING TIME FOR EACH OTHER

At the end of the day, do you ever feel like you need an extra twenty-four hours—some for sleeping, some for reclaiming your favorite pastimes, and plenty for each other? "Couple time" is a real challenge to new parents, who find that the family's new arrival can easily take up both parents' time and attention—twenty-four hours a day, seven days a week.

JUST THE TWO OF US

In our book *Love Life for Parents*, we outlined steps for making time for sex. These steps are also very appropriate for simply making time for each other.[9]

Make a commitment to find time for each other.

. . .

Every person makes time for the things that are most important to him or her—even parents! Remember how important you are to each other—and why you chose each other in the first place.

How long has it been since you had any kind of uninterrupted time together? Right now, look at today's to-do list and the calendar for this week. Carve out some time for your partner. While you may want to hire a baby-sitter and plan a "date," time together as a couple doesn't have to be extravagant. It could be that you need to set aside fifteen minutes each morning or each evening before you go to bed to focus on each other. You may have bloodshot eyes, but do it anyway! It's just that important. If you're having difficulty finding even fifteen minutes, take this next suggestion seriously.

> *A man leaves his father and mother and is joined to his wife, and the two are united into one.*
>
> GENESIS 2:24

Analyze your current time constraints. For one week, keep a record of everything you do throughout the day and how long each activity takes. You may be amazed at how you are investing what little discretionary time you do have. How much time do you spend watching television and videos or surfing the Web? How much time do you spend with family and friends? How much time do you give to household chores? What things could be eliminated or put off?

Do the sheets on your bed have to be changed every week? Do you spend extra time running to the store for diapers because you forgot to get them when you did your grocery shopping yesterday? Analyze the data you have collected; you will probably find blocks of time you can reclaim to free up time for your spouse.

A side benefit to this restructuring of your schedule is that your slowed-down lifestyle will make the time you spend with your baby more calm and measured. The result could be a baby who is less agitated and demanding, which can leave you even more time to focus on your partner.

Set apart time for your spouse. The time you find may be short or long, but the key is to invest it in your marriage. We're talking habits here. Develop the habit of using moments to focus on each other—like extending that kiss for ten seconds when you say good-bye in the morning and hello in the evening, or finding ten minutes a day to talk with each other. A healthy habit for all parents is the habit of having a

---

FIVE GREAT MOMENTS FOR PARENT PARTNERS

- Eat a banana split with two spoons.
- Take a shower together in a candlelit bathroom.
- Write a love note on your steamy mirror.
- Take turns giving each other back rubs.
- Watch a romantic movie together.

. . .

weekly date night. Even when you can't go out for the evening, a stay-at-home dinner date with candlelight after the baby is settled gives you a chance to look each other in the eye for a few minutes. After all, when this baby stage is over, you'll still want to recognize your spouse!

Use your time twice. Look for chores and little things you can do together. Start the tradition of making the bed together each morning, while sharing loving thoughts to carry each other through the day. Complete a chore together like cleaning up the kitchen, or take a walk together with the baby in a stroller. While checking your office e-mail, send your spouse an electronic love note. Do the dishes together in the evening. (If you have older kids, they will be sure to stay clear to avoid being recruited to help with the kitchen cleanup!)

> Every person makes time for the things that are most important to him or her.

Get in the habit of interacting while you're doing something else. Keep the conversation going, even if you do have to change the load of laundry (or a loaded diaper!) at the same time.

Guard your time. If you don't guard the time you've reserved for the two of you as a couple, no one else will. When you are tempted to make a new time commitment, ask yourself two questions: "Will this commitment bring my spouse and me closer together or put distance in our relationship?" and "What can I drop off the calendar if I add something else?" One of the most helpful habits you can ever develop is the habit of saying no to those things that overload your time commitments.

... 7 ...

HEALTHY HABIT #4: TALKING AND LISTENING EFFECTIVELY

If you are like most new parents, you are tired and your time—for yourself and for your spouse—is limited. Taking care of an infant or small child is probably more hands-on work than you'd ever imagined. That baby takes up physical, emotional, and relational energy. So don't be surprised if you seem to be losing your emotional connection with each other. Seven out of ten couples report a decrease in the level of communication after they have a baby. Sadly, half of those couples never regain their previous level of interaction.[10]

When you're tired, your ability to communicate and to deal with conflict is challenged to its ultimate limits. So there's no time like right now to work toward some good communication habits.

TAKE TIME TO TALK

Here's a reality bite: Even though it's definitely harder to deal with each other when you are tired, you won't be able to handle the challenges of becoming parents by communicating in twenty-second sound bites. In order to build a strong foundation, it's important that you make regular communication time a habit.

> Be intentional—and creative—about making the expression of positive feelings a habit.

You've just been working on the "time" question, but there are other issues that bring pressure into the whole communication and conflict arena. Whatever issues you were grappling with as a couple before the baby came along, those difficulties come with you into parenthood. Money, for example, might be one area of conflict. Research indicates that most couples struggle in the area of finances and spending-and-saving decisions. While money is one of the top areas of conflict for couples, parenting issues are a close second as frequent argument starters. We have already observed that marital dissatisfaction and conflict increase when we become parents, so it's not surprising that those dear little ones who made us parents in the first

. . .

place test our ability to communicate and resolve conflict.

But don't despair. All that's called for is a little brushing up on your communication skills. In her book *If You Ever Needed Friends, It's Now,* Dr. Leslie Parrott says studies have found that if couples understand each other's goals, worries, hopes, and fears, as well as the details of each other's day, it protects them from a dramatic upheaval in their relationship.[11] So obviously, the two of you need time to talk through your goals, worries, hopes, and fears at times that are relatively calm—before the day's surprises surface.

The following is our best advice for how you can retool those communication skills and develop habits of real listening and positive communication.

LISTEN FOR FEELINGS

There is never a more important time to listen for feelings than when you've just become parents. Sometimes understanding the hidden messages behind words is hard. Of course, sometimes there are no hidden messages, but as you listen for feelings, you can tell a lot by observing your spouse's body language. Are her arms folded defensively? Did he sigh loudly or suddenly pull away from you? Understanding these, and other nonverbal clues—the stares, glares, and "the look"—is important to real communication with your mate.

Did you know that spoken words are only 7 percent of the overall message? The nonverbal communication makes up 55 percent of the message. Your tone of voice—how you say what you say—makes up 38 percent of the total message.[12]

It's possible to say one thing but underneath be communicating totally different feelings. For example, "Sure, honey, you go on back to sleep and I'll get up with the baby" may actually mean, "Why are you being so selfish and inconsiderate? I got up the last time—it's your turn!" If you're listening for the hidden feelings, you might be able to read the nonverbal cues and get the real message. Then you can talk about it before the situation escalates.

WATCH FOR FILTERS

Have you ever had an experience where what you're trying to say to your partner is very different from what he or she hears?

It's frustrating when you're trying to talk to your spouse and he or she just doesn't get it. It may be a problem of filters. A filter affects what gets through, and in communication, filters can distort the real message or the real feelings. In *Fighting for Your Marriage,* the authors describe four filters: *distraction, emotional states, beliefs and expectations, and difference in style.*[13] As we briefly consider each of these four filters, see if you recognize any of them in your own conversation patterns.

Distraction can be the result of external influences: the baby is crying, the TV is blaring in the background, the computer screen is flashing. Sometimes distraction can derive from internal circumstances: you're just too exhausted to concentrate or you're busy thinking up your own rebuttal to what your spouse is saying. When you realize you're distracted, try saying, "Hey, I'm too tired/busy/distracted to talk about this right now." Or when you realize your partner isn't listening, back up and say in a pleasant way, "Are you listening to me right now?" Better still, before you begin a serious conversation, make sure you have your spouse's attention!

The second communication filter comes from *emotional states*. And as new parents you'll experience a

---

QUICKIE COMMUNICATION HELPERS

- Leave an affectionate Post-it note.
- Leave a loving phone message.
- Send an encouraging e-mail to your partner during the day.
- Choose a secret "I love you" signal. Three hand squeezes means, "I love you." Four hand squeezes means, "I love you back!"
- Wink at your spouse.
- Hug for twenty seconds each day.

lot of them. You may be in a bad mood, tired or discouraged, or your hormones are raging! Think about it. If you are in a negative emotional state, anything your spouse says to you will come to you through that negative filter—you'll perceive everything he or she says in a negative way. Before you know it, you can both be negative. So the key to dealing with this emotional filter is it to let your partner know you're in a bad mood. Then he or she can resist becoming defensive and instead can try to understand or empathize with you.

> **Everyone should be quick to listen, slow to speak and slow to become angry.**
> JAMES 1:19, NIV

If there's an important issue you need to discuss, you may want to set aside another time. Say, "Honey, I'm really frustrated right now because the baby has been fussy all day. I'll be able to listen to you better after I get some sleep. Can we plan to talk about it tomorrow morning?"

The third filter comes from *differing beliefs and expectations*. Remember Rita and Will, whose two sets of parents handled their parenting tasks with such divergent approaches? Rita and Will have different beliefs about what "co-parenting" entails, and therefore both have different expectations.

Expectations not only affect our perceptions but can influence the behavior of others.[14] While Rita was assuming that Will wasn't willing to do his share, Will was thinking, "Why bother? She doesn't appreciate anything I do to help anyway." They both needed to acknowledge and talk about their expectations. They couldn't realize it initially, but Rita and Will shared two important goals: they both wanted to be the best partners and parents they could be, and they both really wanted to work together to make it happen. A little communication was the path to better teamwork as partners in parenting.

The fourth filter is *differences in style*. No doubt you and your spouse come from different family backgrounds. Other influences—gender, cultural, and personality differences—also affect the way we communicate. Will came from a more reserved family where emotions were not readily expressed. Rita's family was very expressive, and each was quick to become emotional and passionate in their conversations. So whenever Rita raised her voice, Will assumed there was a big problem. But actually, many times Rita was just being expressive.

Do any of these communication filters seem vaguely familiar? Snatch some time to discuss these barriers to communication whenever you see them cropping up. This can defuse many misunderstandings and help you truly hear what your spouse is saying.

Now that you're aware of filters and how they can

affect your conversation, let's look at some specific tools for communication.

TIPS FOR TALKING

Practice good communication skills. Your actual words and how you say them are important here—and so is listening. Consider these make-or-break communication tips:

- *Start your sentences with "I."* Then let your statement reflect back on you. For example: "I'm feeling really tired and frustrated right now. The baby was fussy all day, and I need a little love and encouragement. Will you hold me for a little bit?" or "I'm getting too angry. Let's wait and talk about this after I've had a rest."
- *Avoid making "you" statements.* They tend to be attacking. For example, avoid saying, "You're so inconsiderate. Can't you at least put your dirty dishes in the sink?"
- *Skip the "why" questions.* These also tend to be attacking. Stop before you make one, and reword it. Instead of saying, "Why can't you take the baby for a little while and give me a break?" Say, "Honey, I'm pooped. Can you take the baby for a few minutes and let me regroup?"
- *Wipe out absolute words like "never" and "always."*

Statements like "You never listen" or "You always say that!" most likely are overstated and will only get you in trouble.

- *Agree not to attack each other or defend yourself.* This simple pact between you can help you keep your relationship growing and healthy—and it can save a lot of emotional energy.
- *Listen, don't react.* James 1:19 tells us to "be quick to listen, slow to speak, and slow to get angry." Listen to your spouse carefully before reacting.
- *Attack the problem, not each other.* Choose to attack the problem together as the team that you are instead of attacking each other. You'll need this skill for the coming parenting years. Nothing can divide parents like a cunning adolescent determined to get his or her way, so learn now how to build a united front!
- *Generously use the words "thank you" and "please."* We all need to be appreciated, and yet we often forget to express courteous appreciation to the one we've chosen as our mate for life.
- *Give your mate three positive statements each day.* It's basic human nature to focus on and express our negative feelings while holding the tender feelings inside. So you'll have to get intentional—and creative—to make the expression of positive feelings a habit.

TALK ABOUT "US"

Focus on your relationship. That wonderful miracle of a little one so easily snatches center stage. It's quite easy to be consumed with talk about the baby. But take the time to talk about you and your relationship. Set aside times—perhaps that Friday-night dinner together after the little one is sleeping—when the topic of baby is taboo and your conversation centers on your relationship. Affirm the positive aspects and commit to work on areas that need improvement. Share your feelings. Look for ways to affirm your spouse, and keep encouraging each other.

Keep talking to each other, even when you're tired. Your communication is the way you reach out to draw each other close.

...8...

HEALTHY HABIT #5: MAKING YOUR LOVE LIFE A PRIORITY

If you want to have a love life after becoming parents, you have to prioritize sexual intimacy. It's amazing how the arrival of a baby can send sexual intimacy plummeting to the bottom of the priority list. Everything else seems to come first: the baby, the housekeeping, your job, your friends, and even your social life. Sex can become an obligation, or something you just don't think about. So, to get your love life back on the front burner, you'll have to get intentional about it.

HOW LONG HAS IT BEEN?

Dr. Jay Belsky, in his research at the University of Pennsylvania, discovered that many couples make love less frequently after childbirth, cuddle less often, show less overall affection for each other, and may lose physical and emotional connectedness. The affection formerly exchanged between partners now is often given to the baby. A *Parents* magazine survey revealed that parents were more than twice as likely to kiss their new baby as they were to kiss each other.[15]

The first few weeks after the birth of your baby may be a blur. If you're the mother, sex may not even have reappeared on your internal radar screen. In one study, 80 percent of new moms said their sex life deteriorated mainly because they were simply too tired to make love.

> Before you resume sex, decide if you're ready to have another baby and what you are going to do about it if you're not.

Then comes the six-week checkup—when the doctor gives the go-ahead for resuming intercourse. How do couples respond? The husband? He might be rarin' to go—like a bull that's been caged too long. Or he might be turned off, having seen his wife produce that baby—like a "birthing machine"—and then nurse it around the clock—like a "milk factory."

Meanwhile, a wife's body has been through a very traumatic experience, and she might not be as eager to resume sex. To her it can seem like everyone wants something from her. The baby is mauling and sucking on her. She is exhausted; her body hurts. As one mom put it, "Dear, I look forward to when we can be together again, but you need to know my body's not so excited. Even now I know you'd like to touch my breasts, but forget it! They're sore, swollen, and the milk is only for the baby!" Obviously, getting reconnected sexually has its hurdles to overcome.

While every couple is unique, the general rule of thumb is to wait six weeks after childbirth to resume sex. Obviously, this will be less for couples who have adopted (although you might be surprised how the distraction and exhaustion affects the sex life of adoptive parents as well). Sometimes, if the mother has had a C-section or a delivery with complications, the time may be extended.

But even at six weeks, it's important to be sensitive to Mom's feelings. She needs to know that Dad finds her attractive, and she needs a little romance. It's a great time for back rubs and massages. Just holding hands and cuddling can get her in the mood.

BENEFITS OF PRIORITIZING INTIMACY

- Sex is good for your health.
- Regular sex is a stress-buster.
- It will help "affair-proof" your marriage.
- It will help you stay emotionally connected.
- You'll be a good model for your kids.
- You'll have a healthy love life when the kids grow up and leave home.

. . .

While the six-week measure may signal that her body is recovered enough physically to resume sex, it may take longer for Mom to regain her prepregnancy desires. While it's clear that most women are ready for sex within a short period of time, others require a much longer period of recuperation. According to one survey, it can take some as long as nine months to regain their former level of sexual desire.

Other research reveals that seven out of ten couples begin new patterns in their sexual relationship after the baby is born. A year after the baby's arrival, more than half of new parents have not returned to prepregnancy levels of sexual intercourse. Few parents make love as often as they did before the birth of the baby.

In light of all the challenges that a new baby presents to maintaining an exciting love life, you need to take active steps to make your sexual relationship a high priority.

Create your own private space. A great sex life is dependent upon having a place to be intimate. With no privacy there is little romance. If the baby is in your bedroom, you need to have a portable crib in another room as well so you can claim your own private space. If you have other children this may become more of a challenge, but it's one worth surmounting.

Cultivate your own private times. Having a private

space is a start, but you need to figure out how you can get there and use it. Finding time alone is often harder, but it is vital for developing the habit of having a healthy love life. Make it a point to go to bed an hour earlier than usual, and use that time to reconnect with your spouse. If you have older children, evaluate bedtimes (or lack of them), and see how you might need to restructure your family life. And as your children grow up, it's important for them to see you making your own relationship a priority. Watching you care for your marriage will give them a reference for their future romantic relationships, so do what you need to do to find time for your love life.

Become educated lovers. Becoming a great lover is an acquired skill. Never stop learning about each other. Understanding common male and female dif-

---

HOW A BABY CAN ENRICH YOUR LOVE LIFE

Babies remind you that you are one. Each time you look at baby's toes that are just like Dad's or the eyes that are like Mom's, or you hear your child giggle, you realize this baby is here because you love each other.

Babies encourage creativity. Since babies present many obstacles to finding time alone together, you have to find creative ways of getting together. And the very essence of romance thrives on obstacles.

Babies promote appreciation. Because it's more challenging to find time for a love life, you appreciate it more when you make love.

ferences will enhance your love life. Through all the stages of marriage there is something new to learn. Read about and study the stages of lovemaking. Remember that the most important sex organ is your brain. So talk. Being willing to open yourself up to your partner by talking about your sexual relationship will increase the intimacy between you.

Be willing to experiment. Look for ways to be creative in your love life. If you've been married for five years, do you have five years' worth of sexual expertise or one year's expertise repeated five times? Refusing to be creative and try new things will lead to boredom and dissatisfaction. But experimenting must be done with a backdrop of mutual consent, love, and acceptance. We suggest the following four guidelines that have worked well for us:

1. Whatever we try must be mutually acceptable.
2. We're committed always to seek to please the other.
3. We must have privacy when we are exploring and experimenting.
4. We will talk openly about whatever we are trying.[16]

Do the unexpected. Look for ways to be creative and to surprise each other. At this stage of family life, spontaneity is only possible when one of you plans it for the other. If you've always been midnight lovemakers, try morning sex or get home from work for a long lunch hour. Arrange for a baby-sitter and whisk your spouse away for a quick mystery getaway. You may have only a couple hours before the baby needs you again, but that's enough time to be creative. The extra effort you make to be spontaneous will be well worth the reward.

Schedule sex! Plan ahead. Make appointments and write them on your calendar. Have the sitter take your baby for a stroll or somewhere other than your house. One creative couple told us how they made appointments for the middle of the night when all the kids are sleeping and set their "love" alarm.

The great thing about all the adjustments you'll

**ADVICE FROM OTHER NEW PARENTS
ON FINDING TIME FOR SEX**

- "Don't get stuck in a rut. Any time of day or night is an option."
- "We make appointments with each other."
- "Plan ahead. Agree to make love at least once a week—and keep track."
- "We ask someone else to watch the baby at their house for a couple of hours and we stay home together instead of going out."
- "We work to get our baby's sleeping schedule to work better with ours."
- "We swap off baby-sitting with our good friends."
- "Sometimes we awaken before the alarm goes off, and that's the time when we are physically fresh."
- "We turn off the TV and go to bed early."

. . .

make in your physical intimacy during this new-parents time of your life is that you can set the stage for a lifetime of adjustments. After all, the two of you will keep changing, and so will the challenges of your life. If you can create a shared openness and excitement about your sex life now, that's an achievement that promises a lifetime of sizzling sex.

...9...

HEALTHY HABIT #6: GROWING TOGETHER SPIRITUALLY

In partnership with God, the two of you have created a new life. Doesn't that make you stop to consider your life from a spiritual perspective? You look at this amazing little creation—a new life. Perhaps your heart resonates with Psalm 139:14: "Thank you for making me so wonderfully complex! Your workmanship is marvelous—and how well I know it."

Do you look at your baby and wonder what the world will be like for him when he grows up? It can be disconcerting to think about your child outliving you in a world you'll never experience. Becoming a parent is a benchmark time of life, and it typically leads to questions like, *What is life's meaning? Where is this all heading? Can I handle the parenting thing in my own strength?* Maybe you're having similar thoughts.

For us, the arrival of our first child became a time for spiritual reevaluation. First, it was a difficult birth. We had just moved from Germany to Washington State—thousands of miles from family and friends. We were in a military hospital—at least I (Claudia) was in a military hospital. Back then, husbands weren't allowed anywhere near the delivery room! Our baby was in the breech position. He didn't breathe on his own for the first ten minutes of his life, and in that ten minutes my whole life passed before me. Having been raised in a religious family, my natural instinct was to pray. Believe me, I did! Our baby lived, and I set off on a spiritual pilgrimage that eventually led both David and me to a new understanding of God's love, forgiveness, and how to grow together spiritually. We discovered that we didn't have to have all the answers for being parents and partners. But through our new faith in Christ, we could receive the power and strength to deal with whatever life would bring.

> **Thank you for making me so wonderfully complex! Your workmanship is marvelous— and how well I know it.**
>
> PSALM 139:14

Over thirty-five years later, we can state enthusiastically that God has been faithful. Our life hasn't been problem-free. We've faced many obstacles and troubles: health, finances, loss of close family members, and relationship problems. But through it all our faith in our heavenly Father has given us the power to be "more than conquerors" (Romans 8:37, NIV).

Where are you on your own spiritual journey?

Whether you're just starting to explore these spiritual questions or you're both Christians actively pursuing a relationship with God, these points of discussion and follow-through are worth considering as you attempt to grow together spiritually.

What do you believe?

Talk about your core beliefs. What do you believe about life, death, family, and marriage? Why are you on this planet? What is your view of God? If you have already embraced the living God, does the way you are currently living out your life reflect your core beliefs?

If you would like to know more about how to grow spiritually and how to grow closer to God, we'd encourage you to pick up the book *Making Wise Life Choices* by John Trent, a part of the Life Lines series.

Find a church family

Seek out a place of worship with those who share your core beliefs. As you visit various churches, consider how those who are teaching show that they value and uphold the truths of God's message to people—the Bible. Look for a church where the nursery is safe and well-staffed and where there are programs in place for teaching your child in the years ahead. Is there opportunity for you, as an adult, to find friends—perhaps through small groups or other get-togethers? Don't hesitate to ask for a pastor to visit you if you want to ask questions about a church you're interested in. Many churches often have printed material stating their core doctrinal beliefs and outlining the programs available to those who attend.

Find fellowship
Remember the title of that book by Dr. Leslie Parrott: *If Ever You Needed Friends, It's Now* (Zondervan). At this time in your life, support is all-important. You need to glean wisdom from your friends who have children, and you need a place to share what you're learning. Seek out friends—especially other couples—who share your core beliefs. Perhaps the most natural place to do this is through your church, linking up with people you meet in a Sunday school class or signing up for a couple's study group.

Talk to God
Develop the habit of prayer—on your own and with your spouse. There are myriad joys associated with

that new little one of yours. Pour them out to God—saying, "Thank you for this great gift!" At the same time, there are plenty of worries and long-cherished dreams you hold for your child. Share these with God, the one who holds your child's future (and yours!) in his powerful and loving hands.

Learn together

Develop the habit of couple devotions. By devotions, we mean the study of the Bible, which is God's resource of wisdom for living—a lifeline for parents! If it's hard for you to know where to begin, pick up a study booklet at a Christian bookstore; you'll find there's a large selection. You can study topics—like marriage or parenting—or specific books of the Bible—like John or Proverbs. If you get hooked on the Bible, you may want to have both personal devotional time and time with your spouse. You might

---

SCRIPTURE PASSAGES TO READ AND MEMORIZE

- When you want to express your thanks to God: Psalm 100:4-5
- When you need rest: Psalm 23
- When you're worried: Philippians 4:6-7
- When you're afraid: Isaiah 41:10
- When you want to praise God: Psalm 103:1-5
- When you need assurance of forgiveness: Psalm 103:8-12
- When you need wisdom: James 1:5
- When you need to be reminded what love is: 1 Corinthians 13:4-7

. . .

consider using the *Marriage Devotional Bible* (Zondervan), which contains short devotions and marriage check-ups that are great for parents who must grab time in little bites.

Memorizing Scripture together is another great idea. Choose encouraging passages that will remind you of God's faithfulness and strength at times when you're at the end of your rope. Consider writing these out on note cards and reading through them during late-night feedings.

> Seek out friends—especially other couples—who share your core beliefs.

Reach out

Together with your spouse, find a way to serve others. This may seem pretty impossible during those early weeks with a new baby, but soon you'll be able to find ways to serve together. If you like to cook and enjoy company, try inviting someone who seems lonely to have dinner with you. If you're spending a lot of time in the church nursery anyway, sign up for an official place on the staff rotation. If you need ideas for how to get involved, talk with your pastor. Once he gets over the initial shock as he realizes he's got a willing worker on his hands, he'll probably be able to give you a short list of things that need doing within your church family. Find something on that list that fits with your gifts and talents.

. . .

Your spiritual growth, individually and as a couple, is possibly the most important area of your unity as a couple. You'll find that shared spiritual life is like superglue: as you each grow closer to God, you'll draw together in deep and lasting ways. The teaching of the Bible reinforces your commitment as a couple and holds up an unbeatable ideal for loving. Plus, your own dependence on God is the path to parenting beyond human ability. God can fill you with his wisdom and courage. Don't neglect this all-important area of your relationship.

... 10 ...

HEALTHY HABIT #7: LEARNING TO PACE YOURSELF

It takes nine months to birth a baby, but once you bring your bundle of joy home, you need to get ready for the long haul! Typically it takes a minimum of eighteen years to launch a child into adulthood—and a lifetime after that of loving, caring, and praying for him. So it's important to pace yourself and take the long-term view. Realize that when your child leaves the nest, you still want to be in a loving, close relationship with your spouse. Our advice? At the onset of parenting, pace yourself, remembering that you were partners before you were parents. Keep the vision of a life together—even after the kids leave home—before you all the time.

To help you keep that lifelong commitment to your relationship in perspective, we have a few more words of advice.

Just say no

You can't do everything, so it's important to learn how to say no. And you need to learn how to say no as a couple. When our children were young, we made a pact: Neither of us would take on a new responsibility without consulting the other. Then we would discuss three questions:[17]

1. *Is this activity essential?* Would the sky fall in if you didn't do this? (earning a living, taking care of your baby, sleeping, and eating)
2. *Is this activity really important?* Does it help you be a better spouse or parent? (maintaining a healthy diet and getting exercise, taking a parenting class, going to a marriage seminar) Does it please God and provide a way to serve Him? (being involved in a ministry at church or volunteering at a local charity)
3. *Is this activity discretionary?* Is it optional, simply your choice, something you would like to do? (watching TV, surfing the Web, meeting a friend for coffee)

. . .

These three questions helped us avoid getting overcommitted. They can help you avoid spreading yourself too thin, or perhaps they can help you weed out an already overcrowded agenda.

Often a ministry opportunity is the hardest thing for us to say no to. You may already teach Sunday school, do literacy tutoring, or volunteer at a hospital—and these are wonderful things. But you need to look at your ministry commitments as a couple and come up with criteria for what you're going to be involved with. Sometimes you have to turn down a wonderful opportunity to serve someone else because your own family needs to come first.

This is not to say that discretionary activities are off-limits. We all need some time to relax and regroup. But if unimportant activities are clogging up your schedule, it's time to make some changes.

Take care of you
It's important to take care of yourself! While becoming parents is really exciting and positive, in one

---

WORKOUT SHORTCUTS FOR BUSY PARENTS
- Do standing push-ups against the kitchen counter.
- Jump rope.
- Lie on your back and lift your baby instead of weights.
- Go up and down the stairs several times.

> *Teach us to make the most of our time, so that we may grow in wisdom.*
>
> PSALM 90:12

sense you lose your old self. Since transitional times are often so stressful and exhausting, you can lose more of your old self than is necessary or healthy. Stress and fatigue can actually feed each other, so if you're not taking care of yourself, you may be experiencing both! Here are some tips for taking care of you:

- *Take time for yourself.* Even if it's only a few minutes a day, carve out a small block of time that is just for you.
- *Get regular exercise.* We've said it before, but it's important enough that we'll say it again. Even if your partner won't participate, make a way to get some exercise.
- *Watch your diet.* Eating healthy will boost your energy level. Cutting out high-fat foods will make you feel less sluggish. High-energy foods such as pasta, fruit, and yogurt can support you throughout the day.

Get information

It's easy to let your world get as narrow as the four walls of your house—or perhaps your home and your workplace and nothing else. Your involvement with your friends and activities from church are an excellent antidote to this kind of cocooning. There are other ways you can stay connected to the world around you:

- *Stay intellectually stimulated.* If your mind is active, you'll stay in touch with the world outside your home, be a better parent and a better conversationalist with your partner, and improve your self-esteem. Read a weekly news magazine or listen to the news. Pick a topic to research. This could be a current event, a period in history, or an area of spiritual growth or discipline you want to learn more about.
- *Stay informed.* Search out the best resources for parenting and for building your marriage while you parent your kids. We've provided you with our list of top resources at the end of this book.

Get help

Learn to ask for help. We all need support at times, so don't be shy about asking for assistance when you need it. Ask your partner. Ask your friends. Ask an expert. Parenting is not an exact science, and at times we simply need some help and encouragement from others.

Find a support system. Look for a new-parents

support group, and if you can't find one, start your own. You'll have the opportunity to give and receive much support from other parents who are going through the same things you are. If you share your ideas and struggles, you may be amazed at the creative solutions you develop together.

Accept changing roles
Move ahead. Life is lived in seasons, and you've just entered the parenting season. Embrace it. Renegotiate your roles and responsibilities with each other. Whether one parent is home with the baby or both parents are working outside the home, you need to talk about your roles.

Realize that life is long
There are limits to what you can handle—professionally, socially, or personally—while you are giving your best to parenting. Keep in mind that life is long, and if you can't take advantage of every opportunity that comes along right now, there may be a time when your kids are grown when you can. The good news is that when you're committed for the long haul, you can look forward to a future of adventures with the one you love.

... 11 ...

HEALTHY HABIT #8: NURTURING YOUR RELATIONSHIP

Never forget that before you were parents, you were partners and that it is because of your love for each other that you are parents. So our final challenge to you is to develop the habit of nurturing your relationship. Actually, all the previous healthy habits will help you accomplish this, but it's so important we thought we'd emphasize it one last time.

PUT YOUR SPOUSE FIRST

Over the years we have worked with a lot of young families. We tell the parents, "Your kids will wait while you grab some time for your marriage, but your marriage won't wait until your children grow up."

The one thing that concerns us is that parents often put their children before their marriage. Now, we realize that babies take a tremendous amount of time and emotional energy. (We won't even mention the adolescent years.) But we hope you'll keep striving to keep your marriage relationship front and center.

> Marriage is for a lifetime, so our best advice is to take time each day to nurture your relationship.

Parenting is a long but temporary job. Marriage is for a lifetime, so our best advice is to take time each day to nurture your relationship. Your relationship is what you will have when the kids leave home. We suggest three ways to make your marriage a priority.

Encourage one another
Give some encouragement each day. Consistently choose to build up your mate instead of tearing him or her down. It's easy to become critical and to let nitpicking become a regular pattern. It's so easy to let angry words fly, poisoning the atmosphere of peace in your home. Counteract these tendencies by intentionally speaking words of affirmation and expressing affection every day.

Date your mate
Couples who continue or start the dating habit seem to stay emotionally connected over the years. Dates don't

SIMPLE WAYS TO GIVE ENCOURAGEMENT

- Clip a funny cartoon or joke and put it on the refrigerator or bathroom mirror.
- Give your spouse a one-minute shoulder rub.
- Write a note and slip it in your spouse's pocket.
- Say, "Let's not cook dinner tonight" and order pizza.
- Light a candle together.
- Rent a romantic video.
- Rent a funny video!
- Buy your spouse a new CD.
- Pick up a good joke book.
- Plan a candlelit dinner.
- Hold hands.
- Relax with a cup of tea.
- Pray together.

SIMPLE WAYS TO ENCOURAGE HER

- Bring her flowers.
- Clean the bathroom.
- Don't surprise her with unexpected guests.
- Say "I love you" often.
- Scratch her back.
- Score big points by asking daily, "What can I do for you today?"
- Tell her what a great mom she is.

SIMPLE WAYS TO ENCOURAGE HIM

- Focus on him.
- Squeeze his hand.
- Surprise him with a hug.
- Tell him why you're glad he's the father of your baby.
- When he's really exhausted, say, "I'll get the baby; you sleep."
- Give him a foot massage.
- Tell him what a great dad he is.

> Take the moments you do have—as tired and exhausted, sleep deprived, and stressed out as you are—and celebrate your love for each other.

have to be expensive. You can even stay home and have a great date. Plan it for when the baby is sleeping. Set up your own dining-room table as if it were a restaurant, and get take-out food.

Be realistic about your own energy level. One couple we know made the effort to get a sitter for their three children—including a new baby—so they could go out to dinner. Once they arrived at the restaurant, however, they just stared at each other, too exhausted even to talk! A long nap might have done them more good than a night out.

Build your friendship

Our last suggestion is to do whatever you can to build your friendship with one another. In our work in marriage education over the years, we've found (and research confirms) that one of the best indicators of a successful long-term marriage is the level of friendship within the marriage. It's so important. So take the moments you do have—as tired and exhausted, sleep deprived, and stressed out as you are—and celebrate your love for each other. Cultivate your inside jokes. Laugh together as often as possible. Renew your commitment. Children are with us for a season, but your marriage is for a lifetime.

LIFELONG PARTNERSHIP

We hope that you have assimilated some good tips for nurturing your relationship and for feeling more confident as new parents. In these pages we have emphasized your teamwork as a couple, but the very best way to be good parents is to take care of each other first. And don't forget to keep your sense of humor—that may well be your greatest asset in developing the healthy habits you need to nurture your love while you parent your kids.

It takes three weeks to make a new habit and six weeks to feel reasonably good about it, so we challenge you to be proactive about working on these eight healthy habits. In the weeks ahead, choose one healthy habit to concentrate on each week, starting with the ones you feel need the most work and attention.

You can give your baby one of the greatest gifts a parent can give—the opportunity to grow up in a home with parents who love him or her and love each other. It doesn't get any better than that!

... ADDITIONAL RESOURCES ...

SEMINARS AND PROGRAMS

Becoming Parents is an innovative program developed by Pamela Jordan, Ph.D., R.N., associate professor in the Department of Family and Child Nursing, University of Washington. This program is a modified and expanded version of the highly acclaimed Prevention and Relationship Enhancement Program (PREP; see below) and will help you focus on strengthening your marriage before and after you become parents. For more information, see www.becomingparents.com.

The *Marriage Alive Seminar,* developed by David and Claudia Arp, is a six-hour seminar that will help you focus on your marriage and strengthen your relationship. Topics covered include prioritizing your marriage, finding unity in diversity, learning to talk, resolving conflict, cultivating spiritual intimacy, putting more fun in your marriage, and having an intentional marriage. For the current Marriage Alive Seminar schedule or to inquire about hosting a seminar contact www.marriagealive.com.

Mothers of Preschoolers International (MOPS) is a wonderful support for mothers of preschoolers usually offered through local churches. Check their Web site at www.mops.org for a program in your area.

PEP Groups for Parents video-based program developed by the Arps is a small group resource to use in your church or with other parents. For more information contact www.marriagealive.com.

Prevention and Relationship Enhancement Program (PREP) strengthens marriages through better communication.

Seminars and videos are available. Couples who attend workshops learn speaker-listener techniques, problem-solving skills, and a conflict-resolution process. See www.PREPinc.com for additional information.

BOOKS

On Marriage

The 5 Love Needs of Men and Women by Gary and Barbara Rosberg

10 Great Dates to Energize Your Marriage by David and Claudia Arp. Ten fun dates with discussion starters that will help you learn skills to strengthen your marriage relationship in the context of a date night. Video curriculum is also available and can be used in a group setting. Your church might want to consider providing child care so that couples who attend the sessions can have an evening out to build their relationship. For more information, see www.marriagealive.com or call 1-888-690-6667.

52 Dates for You and Your Mate by David and Claudia Arp. Dating suggestions for couples who want to spend fun-focused time together.

Communication and Conflict Resolution in Marriage by Norman Wright

Fighting for Your Marriage: Positive Steps for a Loving and Lasting Relationship by Howard J. Markman, Scott M. Stanley, and Susan L. Blumberg

The Good Marriage by Judith S. Wallerstein and Sandra Blakeslee

The Heart of Commitment: Compelling Research That Reveals the Secrets of a Lifelong, Intimate Marriage by Scott Stanley

A Lasting Promise by Scott Stanley et al. This is a Christian edition of *Fight for Your Marriage*.

Love Life for Parents by David and Claudia Arp. Practical helps for busy parents who want to renew intimacy, romance, and fun.

Marriage Devotional Bible—David and Claudia Arp, Les and Leslie Parrott, and Bob and Rosemary Barnes, editors. Contains short devotions to help you focus on your marriage and easy-to-do marriage checkups.

We Can Work It Out: Making Sense of Marital Conflict by Clifford Notarius and Howard J. Markman

On the Transition to Parenting

After the Baby: Making Sense of Marriage after Childbirth by Rhonda Kruse Nordin. This book offers practical and readable advice that will help strengthen your marriage following the birth of a baby.

And Baby Makes Four by Hilory Wagner. Tips on how to prepare for and welcome a second child into the family.

Becoming Parents by Pamela L. Jordan, Howard J. Markman, and Scott M. Stanley

If You Ever Needed Friends, It's Now by Leslie Parrott

When Husband and Wife become Mom and Dad by Elisa Morgan and Carol Kuykendall

On Child Development

Child Behavior by Frances L. Ilg, Louise Bates Ames, and Sidney M. Baker. The classic child-care manual from the Gesell Institute of Human Development.

Complete Book of Baby and Child Care by Focus on the Family

What to Expect the First Year by Arlene Eisenberg, Heidi E. Murkoff, and Sandee E. Hathaway

VIDEOS

10 Great Dates to Energize Your Marriage by David and Claudia Arp. (See information in Books section.)

Fighting for Your Marriage: The PREP Approach by Scott Stanley, Howard Markman, and Susan Blumberg. Videotape series published by PREP Educational Videos, Inc.: Denver, Colorado. For more information, call 1-800-366-0166 or see www.PREPinc.com

WEB SITES

America's Family Coaches . . . LIVE!—www.afclive.com

Focus on the Family—www.family.org

Marriage Alive International, Inc.—www.marriagealive.com

Mothers of Preschoolers (MOPS)—www.mops.org

Smalley Relationship Center—www.smalleyonline.com

Coalition for Marriage, Family, and Couples Education—www.smartmarriages.com

. . . ENDNOTES . . .

1 Leslie Parrott, *If You Ever Needed Friends, It's Now* (Grand Rapids, Mich.: Zondervan Publishing House, 2000), 79.
2 Pamela L. Jordan, Scott M. Stanley, and Howard J. Markman, *Becoming Parents* (San Francisco: Jossey-Bass, 1999), xi.
3 Ibid., xiii.
4 Rhonda Kruse Nordin, *After the Baby: Making Sense of Marriage after Childbirth* (Dallas: Taylor Publishing Co., 2000), 27.
5 Ibid., 29.
6 Ibid., 31.
7 Ibid., 82.
8 Jordan et al., *Becoming Parents*, 210–216.
9 David and Claudia Arp, *Love Life for Parents* (Grand Rapids, Mich.: Zondervan, 1998), 89–93.
10 Nordin, *After the Baby*, 130.
11 Parrott, *If You Ever Needed Friends, It's Now*.
12 Norman Wright, *Communication and Conflict Resolution in Marriage* (Elgin, Ill.: David C. Cook, 1977), 6.
13 Howard J. Markman, Scott M. Stanley, and Susan L. Blumberg, *Fighting for Your Marriage* (San Francisco: Jossey-Bass, l994), 93.
14 Ibid., 96.
15 Nordin, *After the Baby*, 124.
16 Arp and Arp, *Love Life for Parents*, 131.
17 Arp and Arp, *Love Life for Parents*, 100.

... MARRIAGE ALIVE INTERNATIONAL ...

Marriage Alive International, Inc., founded by husband-wife team Claudia and David Arp, MSW, is a nonprofit marriage- and family-enrichment ministry dedicated to providing resources, seminars, and training to empower churches to help build better marriages and families. The Arps are marriage and family educators, popular speakers, award-winning authors, and frequent contributors to print and broadcast media. They have appeared as marriage experts on programs such as *Today, CBS This Morning,* and *Focus on the Family*. Their Marriage Alive seminar is in great demand across the U.S. and in Europe.

The Mission of Marriage Alive is to identify, train, and empower leaders who invest in others by building strong marriage and family relationships through the integration of biblical truth, contemporary research, practical application, and fun.

Our Resources and Services
- Marriage and family books and small-group resources
- Video-based educational programs including *10 Great Dates to Energize Your Marriage* and *Second Half of Marriage*
- Marriage, pre-marriage, and parenting seminars, including *Before You Say "I Do," Marriage Alive, Second Half of Marriage,* and *Empty Nesting*
- Coaching, mentoring, consulting, training, and leadership development

CONTACT MARRIAGE ALIVE INTERNATIONAL AT WWW.MARRIAGEALIVE.COM OR (888) 690-6667.

... SMALLEY RELATIONSHIP CENTER ...

The Smalley Relationship Center, founded by Dr. Gary Smalley, offers many varied resources to help people strengthen their marriage and family relationships. The Center provides marriage enrichment products, conferences, training material, articles, and clinical services—all designed to make your most important relationships *successful* relationships.

The Mission of the Smalley Relationship Center is to increase marriage satisfaction and lower the divorce rate by providing a deeper level of care. We want to help couples build strong, successful, and satisfying marriages.

Resources and Services:
- Nationwide conferences: Love Is a Decision, Marriage for a Lifetime
- Counseling services: Couples Intensive program, phone counseling
- Video series, including *Keys to Loving Relationships, Homes of Honor,* and *Secrets to Lasting Love*
- Small group leadership guide
- Articles on marriage, parenting, and stepfamilies
- Smalley Counseling Center provides counseling, national intensives, and more for couples in crisis

CONTACT SMALLEY RELATIONSHIP CENTER AT WWW.SMALLEYONLINE.COM OR 1-800-84-TODAY.